# John Cabot & Son

by David Goodnough
illustrated by Allan Eitzen

**Troll Associates**

**Troll Associates, Mahwah, N.J.**
Library of Congress Catalog Card Number: 78-18054
ISBN 0-89375-172-3
ISBN 0-89375-164-2 Paper Edition

# John Cabot & Son

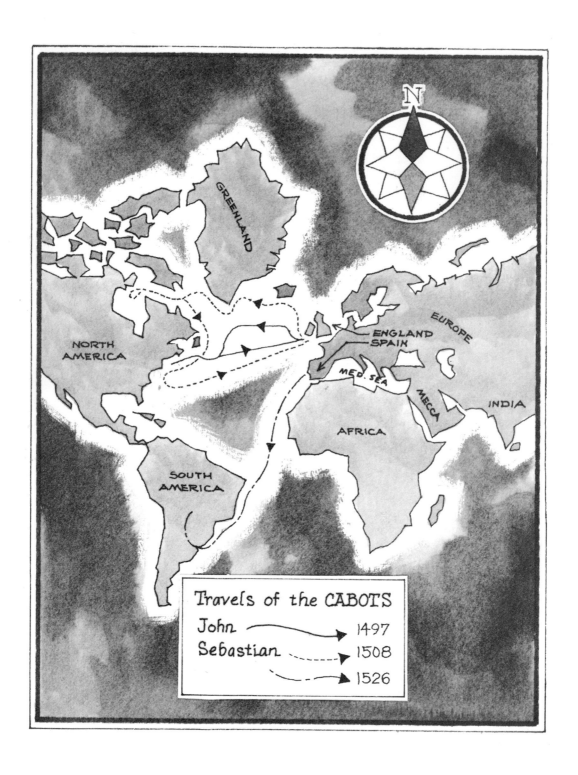

The city of Genoa, Italy, is famous as the birthplace of Christopher Columbus. But another great explorer was born there in 1450, just a year before the birth of Columbus. His name was John Cabot, and he was to play an important part in the discovery and settlement of North America.

John Cabot lived in Genoa only until he was 10, but by that time the sea was the most important thing in his life. He often sailed along the coast of the Mediterranean with his father. He loved watching the great trading ships as they sailed in and out of the harbor.

5

Then his family moved to Venice in about 1461. And Venice was even more exciting than Genoa. The Venetians owned the greatest fleet of ships in Europe. Here sailors and merchants from many lands jostled one another in the narrow streets. Young John quickly became accustomed to hearing the sound of many strange languages.

He loved running errands for his mother, for this meant he could move among the sailors as they swapped tales of wonderful adventures and dangerous sea voyages. The sailors told of thundering winds and snapping sails, of waves as high as mountains and of frightening sea monsters. They tried to outdo each other with stories of the strange people and customs in faraway places across the Mediterranean Sea.

7

Most of all, John loved to watch as great chests were unloaded from the Venetian ships in the harbor. Inside these chests were rich spices, silks, ivory, and rare jewels. His father told him that these came from a mysterious, far-off part of the world called the East Indies—India, China, and Japan.

At that time, the Arab countries controlled almost all the lands that surrounded the Mediterranean Sea. In fact, no ship could sail the Mediterranean without their permission. The merchants of Venice had the greatest fleet of ships in Europe. So the Arabs gave them permis-

8

sion to carry all the spices, silks, and gems from the Far East and take them to Venice. From there they took their precious cargoes to different parts of Europe and traded them for cloth, wood, and metals—materials the Arab countries needed.

9

Since Venice was the only state in Europe that could trade with the Arabs, Venetian merchants could charge as much as they liked for their valuable cargoes. The other seafaring countries of Europe thought this was unfair, and they were beginning to search for other routes to Asia. They wanted to bypass the Mediterranean Sea and deal directly with the countries of the Far East. They, too, wanted the wealth from India, China, and Japan.

John tried to imagine how camel caravans traveled over thousands of miles to bring the rich cargoes from the Indies. The caravans brought the cargoes to Mecca, a great inland trading center, and from there to the ports along the edges of the Mediterranean Sea.

10

But where *was* Asia? What was it like? Was it true, as some said, that a ship could travel by water to reach the Indies?

All that Europeans of John Cabot's time knew about Asia was what they learned by reading the books of Marco Polo. He had traveled to China by an overland route more than 200 years earlier. Marco Polo had described rich cities and palaces in Asia, and the island of *Cipango*, which was later called Japan.

In the 1400's, many people thought that the great continent Marco Polo had explored stretched far to the northeast, where it ended in a point. They believed that the caravans must come from the very farthest part of Asia—perhaps even from Cipango.

But they were wrong. The spices came from the islands off the southeast coast of Asia and from the west coast of India. People in Europe did not have any way of knowing this. Portuguese mariners had not yet sailed around the southern tip of Africa and discovered the water route to the Spice Islands and India. Until this happened in 1498, the spices had to be shipped by land, across the long caravan routes to Mecca.

By the early 1480's, John Cabot had become an experienced seaman, navigator, and mapmaker. Now he commanded a ship of his own, and he had sailed many times to trading ports in the Mediterranean.

But Cabot was curious about exactly *where* his cargoes came from. Once, he left his ship in the harbor of Alexandria and traveled secretly by land to Mecca. Mecca was a holy city to most of the people of the Arab world. Outsiders were not allowed there. But by wearing a disguise, Cabot was able to see this famous city for himself.

When he got there, he covered his face carefully. The dusty marketplace was crowded with camels, camel drivers, and traders. A caravan had just come in. Cabot wandered around the noisy, sunbaked square. What a strange part of the world this was, and how different from his own. Still, when he returned to his ship, he knew very little more about the world than before his arrival in Mecca.

But during his long sea voyages, Cabot had a lot of time to read and study the ideas of other mariners. Christopher Columbus and many geographers of the time believed that the earth must be shaped like a globe. John Cabot believed this, too. But he thought that both the world and the Atlantic Ocean were much smaller than they really are. He was convinced that Asia was a continent that covered most of the world. He also believed that there was only a short stretch of ocean between western Europe and Asia. "If this is so," he wondered, "then why can't the spices and silks be brought directly across the ocean from Asia to Europe?"

This was a fairly new idea. The Portuguese had been exploring the coast of Africa for several years. They believed that the way to reach Asia was to sail south around Africa and then eastward. But both Cabot and Columbus believed it would be easier for a ship to sail *west* to reach the lands of Asia and the Indies.

By 1484, John Cabot had taken his wife and three young sons to Bristol, England. He had learned that the English were eager to find new lands and fishing grounds. In England, he quickly found work making charts and maps. His sons learned English without much difficulty. And, like their father, they had a deep interest in the sea. Sebastian, in particular, showed signs of becoming an expert navigator and mapmaker.

John Cabot was eager to test his plan to find a westward route to Asia. He had already approached King Ferdinand of Spain and King John II of Portugal with his idea. But they had not been willing to give him the money for such a voyage. Christopher Columbus himself had been refused help by Portugal and England. Only after much persuasion had Spain's Queen Isabella financed his famous 1492 expedition.

Although Cabot joined in the celebration that welcomed Columbus back from that first successful voyage, he must have felt a little jealous. Now it was being said that Columbus had discovered the ocean route to Asia. *Could that really be true*?

Cabot believed there was an even shorter route than the one Columbus had taken. He meant to cross the Atlantic farther north. He knew that many English sea captains had explored the northern seas in their search for new lands and fishing areas. They had already given him valuable information about that part of the world.

22

Finally, he was able to convince Bristol's most important merchants that his plan was a good one. They agreed to supply him with a fleet of ships. All he needed now was the permission of the king of England. Without this permission, called a *royal charter*, Cabot could not claim any of his discoveries for England. They would be free for the taking by any European country.

John Cabot went to London to ask for the king's help. King Henry VII, known as a penny pincher, had turned down Christopher Columbus' request for money for a fleet of ships. The king did not want to miss a chance like that again! He quickly gave John Cabot a charter to discover new lands and sources of trade.

Cabot hurried back to Bristol to prepare for his voyage. But he found that, instead of the fleet he expected, he was given one small ship named the *Matthew*. But this did not discourage Cabot—his hopes were high—and he set sail on May 2, 1497. With him was a crew of 18 men. The tiny ship sailed bravely out of Bristol Channel and around the southern coast of Ireland. Then it headed into the stormy and treacherous northern ocean.

Five weeks later, an excited sailor called out, "Land ho!" The men crowded the rails. Was it one of the islands that seamen believed to be in the middle of the ocean? Was it the fabled Cipango? Or could it be the coast of China itself? Cabot approached the mysterious land carefully.

It was a rugged shore, and there were many rocks hidden just beneath the surface of the water. If Cabot was straining his eyes to see the golden domes and jeweled palaces of the East, he was soon disappointed. He was gazing on a wilderness.

It is not known exactly where John Cabot first sighted land. Some think it was Cape Breton Island, near Newfoundland. Others believe it was at the very northern tip of Newfoundland. But wherever it was, Cabot did not drop anchor right away. He sailed along the coast until he found a good landing place, and then took a few men ashore. In a short ceremony, he planted the banner of King Henry VII in the ground, and claimed the land for England.

Cabot and his sailors explored inland for a short distance. They did not see any people or animals, but they did notice that trees had been cut. They

found the remains of some campfires. They also found traps for capturing small animals and a painted stick with holes drilled at both ends. This was probably an Indian tool for making fishing nets.

Cabot was becoming more convinced that he had made a major discovery, so he set out to explore the coastline. At one place, he saw land that seemed to have been cleared for farming or grazing. At another, his men spotted moving figures, but they could not tell whether they were people.

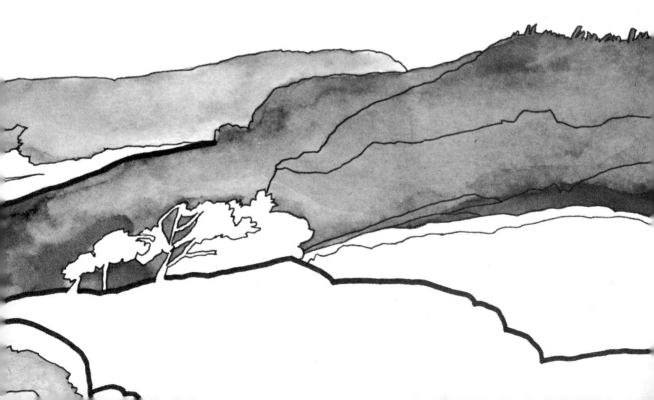

What Cabot did notice was the great number of fish. The waters were filled with so many fish that at times the ship could hardly get through. Cabot later reported that all a person had to do was to lower a weighted basket into the water and haul it up full of fish.

Next, John Cabot sailed to the southern tip of the island and found deep, open water to the west. He was sure he had found an island off the coast of Asia, and that the huge continent lay just over the horizon. However, with only one ship and few men, he did not feel prepared to go any farther. He decided to return to England. He knew he would have no trouble getting a fleet for a second trip—this one to be a grand voyage of discovery! The *Matthew* sailed back into Bristol Harbor on August 6, 1497, eleven weeks after its departure.

John Cabot was given a joyful greeting, and word of his "new found land" spread quickly. Cabot proudly reported his discovery to the merchants. Then he left for London to inform the king.

Although Cabot had only a painted stick and a few animal traps to show for his voyage, King Henry was very impressed by the report of good land, a mild climate, and excellent fishing areas. He rewarded Cabot with a large sum of money. All England now called John Cabot "The Great Admiral." Filled with pride—and no doubt feeling he had equaled Christopher Columbus' triumph— Cabot immediately began to plan for a new expedition.

King Henry lost no time in granting Cabot a second charter. He also gave Cabot permission to form a colony in Cipango, and instructed him to set up a trading center for collecting and shipping spices to England. The king provided one ship and Bristol merchants supplied four more ships for the voyage. In May of 1498, John Cabot sailed once again from Bristol Harbor—this time with even greater hope and confidence.

At sea, one of the ships in the fleet had trouble and turned back for repairs. Cabot and the other four ships sailed on into the great, dark ocean.

They were never seen again.

John Cabot's last voyage remains a mystery. Did he ever reach the land of his first discovery and sail beyond it to find more new lands? Or did he perish at sea before reaching his "new found land?"

No one knows.

By the early 1500's, Europeans were beginning to realize that the land Christopher Columbus and John Cabot had believed to be Asia might instead be *another* continent—in addition to Europe, Asia, and Africa. So it is not surprising that in 1508, Sebastian Cabot—a skilled navigator and mapmaker like his father—set out from Bristol with two ships to explore the great mass of land to the west of Europe.

Sebastian set his course to the north. He sailed so far that he sighted large floating icebergs, even though it was July. Then he found what appeared to be open sea to the west. This might have been the strait that leads into Canada's Hudson Bay. Sebastian believed that he could sail through it to Asia, but his sailors refused to go any farther. Threatened with mutiny, Sebastian had to turn back. But he was certain that he had found a Northwest Passage to Asia.

Now Sebastian set a course to the south. He made a long cruise down the coast of almost all of North America. He explored many bays and inlets, and made contact with some of the Indians who lived there. He may have sailed as far south as Florida, seeking a southern route to Asia. But then he turned back again toward Europe.

After a good return voyage, Sebastian arrived in England in 1509 to learn some important news. King Henry VII had died, and his son, Henry VIII, had taken his place.

The new king was not interested in exploration or discovery. Sebastian longed to be at sea again, or at least to plan those voyages to far-off lands that he dreamed of. So he offered his services to Spain as a pilot and mapmaker. For a long while, he did not go to sea. He instructed others in piloting—the actual sailing and navigation of a ship. Later, he was made chief pilot of Spain, responsible for keeping all maps and charts up to date.

Even while he was living in Spain, Sebastian continued to try to get the king of England to let him search for the Northwest Passage through North America. But the king refused to give Sebastian his support.

The years went by. Sebastian became desperate. He wanted to sail and explore once again. He dreamed of the fame and riches that might be his if he discovered new lands. Finally, he was able to convince the Spanish government that he could find a southern route to Asia—an easier and safer route than the one Magellan had found in 1520. At last, in 1526, Sebastian Cabot set sail with four ships.

The Spanish merchants who paid for this expedition wanted Sebastian to sail to the Spice Islands in the East Indies. They wished to open up the best trading route for the rich spice trade there.

44

Instead, Sebastian deliberately headed for the east coast of South America. He had heard tales of great wealth. He spent nearly four years sailing in and out of harbors and inlets, looking for the gold and jewels he believed were there. But he searched in vain.

In 1530, he finally returned to Spain in disgrace. He was found guilty of disobeying orders. Later, when he was invited to return to England and serve the king once again, Sebastian quickly agreed. He was happy to go back to the country where he and his father had found fame and success.

Sebastian Cabot spent the rest of his life in England. There he kept busy at his old trade of mapmaking. He also helped to equip voyages of discovery, and he advised the king on many seagoing expeditions. He remained a lively figure in London until his death in 1557.

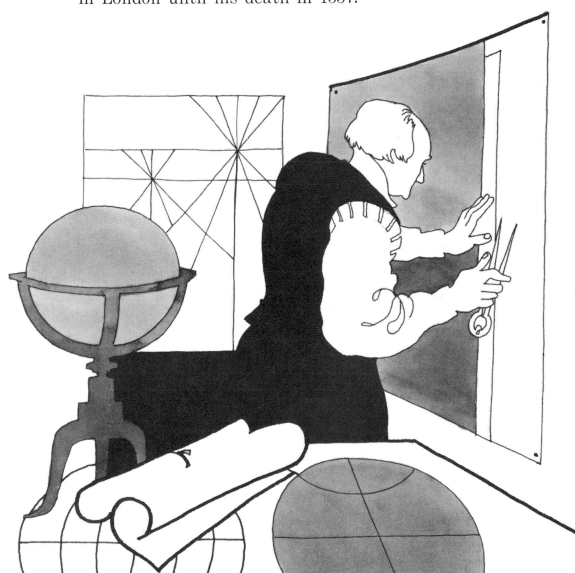

Like John Cabot, Sebastian was a courageous explorer and a mariner of unusual skill. Both father and son devoted their lives to the discovery of new lands and seas. When the English first settled the North American continent at Jamestown, Virginia, in 1607, they did so on land that they could claim as English territory by right of discovery—thanks to John and Sebastian Cabot.

# THE TALE OF
# SQUIRREL NUTKIN

# THE TALE OF
# SQUIRREL NUTKIN

## BY
## BEATRIX POTTER

## A LITTLE SIMON BOOK

Published by Simon & Schuster, Inc.
New York

The Tale of Peter Rabbit
The Tale of Squirrel Nutkin
The Tale of Benjamin Bunny
The Tale of Tom Kitten
The Tale of Mrs. Tiggy-Winkle
The Tale of Jemima Puddle-Duck
The Tale of the Flopsy Bunnies
The Tailor of Gloucester

Created and manufactured by arrangement with Ottenheimer Publishers, Inc.

Copyright © 1986 by Ottenheimer Publishers, Inc.

Published by LITTLE SIMON, a division of Simon & Schuster, Inc., Simon & Schuster
Building, 1230 Avenue of the Americas, New York, New York 10020, by arrangement
with Ottenheimer Publishers, Inc.

Printed under license from Frederick Warne & Co.

**Little Simon and colophon are trademarks of Simon & Schuster, Inc.**

Printed in Italy.

10  9  8  7  6  5  4  3  2  1

ISBN: 0-671-62926-3

# A STORY FOR NORAH

THIS is a Tale about a tail—
a tail that belonged to a
little red squirrel, and his name
was Nutkin.

He had a brother called
Twinkleberry, and a great many
cousins: they lived in a wood
at the edge of a lake.

IN the middle of the lake there is an island covered with trees and nut bushes; and amongst those trees stands a hollow oak-tree, which is the house of an owl who is called Old Brown.

ONE autumn when the nuts were ripe, and the leaves on the hazel bushes were golden and green—Nutkin and Twinkle-berry and all the other little squirrels came out of the wood, and down to the edge of the lake.

THEY made little rafts out of twigs, and they paddled away over the water to Owl Island to gather nuts.

Each squirrel had a little sack and a large oar, and spread out his tail for a sail.

THEY also took with them an offering of three fat mice as a present for Old Brown, and put them down upon his door-step.

Then Twinkleberry and the other little squirrels each made a low bow, and said politely—

"Old Mr. Brown, will you favour us with permission to gather nuts upon your island?"

BUT Nutkin was excessively impertinent in his manners. He bobbed up and down like a little red *cherry*, singing—

"Riddle me, riddle me, rot-tot-tote!
A little wee man, in a red red coat!
A staff in his hand, and a stone in his
    throat;
If you'll tell me this riddle, I'll give you
    a groat."

Now this riddle is as old as the hills; Mr. Brown paid no attention whatever to Nutkin.

He shut his eyes obstinately and went to sleep.

THE squirrels filled their little sacks with nuts, and sailed away home in the evening.

BUT next morning they all came back again to Owl Island; and Twinkleberry and the others brought a fine fat mole, and laid it on the stone in front of Old Brown's doorway, and said—

"Mr. Brown, will you favour us with your gracious permission to gather some more nuts?"

23

24

BUT Nutkin, who had no respect, began to dance up and down, tickling old Mr. Brown with a *nettle* and singing—

"Old Mr. B! Riddle-me-ree!
Hitty Pitty within the wall,
Hitty Pitty without the wall;
If you touch Hitty Pitty,
Hitty Pitty will bite you!"

Mr. Brown woke up suddenly and carried the mole into his house.

HE shut the door in Nutkin's face. Presently a little thread of blue *smoke* from a wood fire came up from the top of the tree, and Nutkin peeped through the key-hole and sang—

"A house full, a hole full!
And you cannot gather a bowl-full!"

THE squirrels searched for nuts all over the island and filled their little sacks.

But Nutkin gathered oak-apples —yellow and scarlet—and sat upon a beech-stump playing marbles, and watching the door of old Mr. Brown.

ON the third day the squirrels got up very early and went fishing; they caught seven fat minnows as a present for Old Brown.

They paddled over the lake and landed under a crooked chestnut tree on Owl Island.

32

TWINKLEBERRY and six other little squirrels each carried a fat minnow; but Nutkin, who had no nice manners, brought no present at all. He ran in front, singing—

"The man in the wilderness said to me,
'How many strawberries grow in the sea?'
I answered him as I thought good—
'As many red herrings as grow in the wood.'"

But old Mr. Brown took no interest in riddles—not even when the answer was provided for him.

ON the fourth day the squirrels brought a present of six fat beetles, which were as good as plums in *plum-pudding* for Old Brown. Each beetle was wrapped up carefully in a dock-leaf, fastened with a pine-needle pin.

But Nutkin sang as rudely as ever—

"Old Mr. B! riddle-me-ree
Flour of England, fruit of Spain,
Met together in a shower of rain;
Put in a bag tied round with a string,
If you'll tell me this riddle, I'll give you a
ring!"

Which was ridiculous of Nutkin, because he had not got any ring to give to Old Brown.

THE other squirrels hunted up and down the nut bushes; but Nutkin gathered robin's pin-cushions off a briar bush, and stuck them full of pine-needle pins.

ON the fifth day the squirrels brought a present of wild honey; it was so sweet and sticky that they licked their fingers as they put it down upon the stone. They had stolen it out of a bumble *bees'* nest on the tippitty top of the hill.

But Nutkin skipped up and down, singing—

"Hum-a-bum! buzz! buzz! Hum-a-bum buzz!
As I went over Tipple-tine
I met a flock of bonny swine;
Some yellow-nacked, some yellow backed!
They were the very bonniest swine
That e'er went over Tipple-tine."

OLD Mr. Brown turned up his eyes in disgust at the impertinence of Nutkin.

But he ate up the honey!

THE squirrels filled their little
sacks with nuts.

But Nutkin sat upon a big flat
rock, and played ninepins with a
crab apple and green fir-cones.

ON the sixth day, which was Saturday, the squirrels came again for the last time; they brought a new-laid *egg* in a little rush basket as a last parting present for Old Brown.

But Nutkin ran in front laughing, and shouting—

"Humpty Dumpty lies in the beck,
With a white counterpane round his neck,
Forty doctors and forty wrights,
Cannot put Humpty Dumpty to rights!"

NOW old Mr. Brown took an interest in eggs; he opened one eye and shut it again. But still he did not speak.

NUTKIN became more and more impertinent—

"Old Mr. B! Old Mr. B!
Hickamore, Hackamore, on the King's
kitchen door;
All the King's horses, and all the
King's men,
Couldn't drive Hickamore, Hackamore,
Off the King's kitchen door."

Nutkin danced up and down like a *sunbeam*; but still Old Brown said nothing at all.

NUTKIN began again—

"Arthur O'Bower has broken his band,
He comes roaring up the land!
The King of Scots with all his power,
Cannot turn Arthur of the Bower!"

Nutkin made a whirring noise to sound like the *wind,* and he took a running jump right onto the head of Old Brown! . . . .

Then all at once there was a flutterment and a scufflement and a loud "Squeak!"

The other squirrels scuttered away into the bushes.

WHEN they came back very cautiously, peeping round the tree—there was Old Brown sitting on his door-step, quite still, with his eyes closed, as if nothing had happened.

\*    \*    \*    \*    \*

*But Nutkin was in his waist-coat pocket!*

THIS looks like the end of the story; but it isn't.

OLD BROWN carried Nutkin into his house, and held him up by the tail, intending to skin him; but Nutkin pulled so very hard that his tail broke in two, and he dashed up the staircase and escaped out of the attic window.

AND to this day, if you meet Nutkin up a tree and ask him a riddle, he will throw sticks at you, and stamp his feet and scold, and shout—

"Cuck-cuck-cuck-cur-r-r-cuck-k-k!"

THE END

Potter, Beatrix copy 2
The Tale of Squirrel
Nutkin

| DATE DUE | | | |
|----------|---|---|---|
| Mar.15,07 | | | |
| | | | |
| | | | |
| | | | |
| | | | |
| | | | |
| | | | |
| | | | |
| | | | |
| | | | |
| | | | |

"My, what a lot of books," said Lamont, as
he went into the library. "Here's an interest-
ing looking one called 'Open Here'."

As Lamont pulled the book from the shelf,
a hidden panel in the book shelf creaked
open and there stood — a pair of ghosts!

"It's Uriah the Heap!" they screamed
as they disappeared.

"If people confuse me with that terrible
fellow," said Lamont, "I'll never find a friend."

Lamont walked down the hall until he came to a
door where a lot of smoke was seeping out.

Disregarding the sign on the door, he opened
it to see what was inside.

"Awwwkkkk!" shrieked the witch. "How dare you
interrupt me when I'm mixing my secret potion!"

"Sorry, dear," whimpered Lamont. "I was
just looking for a friend."

"Begone!" cried the Witch. "And may
you meet Uriah the Heap
before the day's out!
He'll take care of you!"

"That's what I'm afraid of,"
shuddered Lamont as he crept away.

"I'll try one more door before I give up and go home," said Lamont as he stopped before the largest door in the house.

The lonely monster should have been more careful, but he was willing to risk anything to find a friend. He reached out and threw open the door, only to find— Uriah the Heap!

"Aha!" cried the horrible Heap. "It looks like I've found another victim!"

Open

"P-p-p-please, Mr. Heap," Lamont stammered.
"I'd make a terrible breakfast. Couldn't we be friends?"

"Friends?" cried Uriah the Heap. "Friends?!?
You and me? Friends?!?!"

"Well, that *is* why I came here, Mr. Heap.
I want so much to have a friend."

And at that, a great big, shiny tear
trickled down the cheek of Uriah the Heap. "No
one has ever wanted to be my friend before,"
he said. "This is the happiest day of my horrible life!"
All the other creatures, who were lurking in
the fireplace, could hardly believe their ears.